A TRYST WITH WORDS

A Collection of Poems

AKSHARA RAJESH

BookLeaf Publishing

India | USA | UK

Made with ❤ on the BookLeaf Publishing Platform
www.bookleafpub.in
www.bookleafpub.com

Dedication

*"A day never passed, without your stride,
All my journey is your pride, a word in 'thanks',
Is too short a syllable, for your love is oceans deep,
This book is an ode, an embrace to your endless guide."*

To Paappu, Amma and Acha - for their unwavering support and trust in me.

Preface

Is this destiny? Or a mere coincidence? It is neither, it is the echoes of your hard work and perseverance. This book is an answer to millions of people out there, to not suppress your emotions, to not question your ability, an ode to believe in yourself, and a guide to love yourself. Each poem is that part of a shooting star, that one might have failed to catch or if caught, might have let it go, or have caught it to share and embrace. It is an ensemble of dreams, emotions, success and failure, urge to rise and above all, to accept your 'self'. It is the poet's train to reach millions of hearts, and touch their soul. An attempt to say 'You are not alone' and 'You are strong.'

Acknowledgements

Words are less to express gratitude to all my dear ones, who have supported and encouraged me throughout. I thank everyone, who has made this dream come true. A special thanks to my Amma, Acha and Paappu, without whom this journey would have been impossible. Your faith and trust in me are beyond skies, limitless and ever-present. Also, a special thanks to my cousins and friends for their epic shoutouts and appreciations. Each 'Kudos' ignited a new spirit in me to thrive.

Thank You.

1. ECHOES OF POETRY

Well, I heard someone say,
Poetry is a genre that is great,
these magical lines, not a usual phrase,
But it bore in my mind, a hope, a ray,
Of people recognizing that which creates,
Those seraphic verses, a poet's grace.

I smiled a little, a memory to behold,
For those lines were a mirror,
That reflected my soulful self,
I knew, this was a story to be retold,
Not to be forgotten, but to be held nearer,
By all the poets, an exquisite wealth.

Well, someone heard the poetry's echoes,
small, yet an unspoken kindness,
All emotion shared in dearth of words,
one line, they might say, but power it bestows,
Is an unbridled vastness,
A feeling of love it stirred,

For, I heard someone say,
Poetry is a genre that is great.

2. ANKLETS THAT DANCED

The anklets danced to her soulful beats,
each rhythm humming a song so deep,
her heart asking a question, a dream to keep,
Is this her destiny? Or a doleful defeat.
Drifting along with the nature's zephyr
Forgetting her flaunting grief,
A chance given by Eden to reprieve,
To dance without symphony, to wander and linger.
Her eyes travelled along with her hands,
Yet it searched for a realm to stay,
A place for her dreams, a melodic ray,
So serene, so ethereal, a palace so grand.
The cassette of songs, stopped to play,
But, the nature's hymn continued its chime,
Each rhythm of her dance blending with time,
An ecstasy, a joy and not a moment to betray.
The anklets endlessly danced to her soulful beats,
each rhythm humming a song so deep,

her heart asking a question, a dream to keep,
Is this her destiny? Or a doleful defeat.

3. FAMILIAR UNFAMILIARITY

Amidst the fun, fake-ness, frustration,
breathing among the
astounding white and raging black,
aiming to blend in the pool of familiar unfamiliarity,
steadily by leaps and bounds,
enjoining the minute knowledge,
glittering in the pressure of passion,
yet unseeming obliviousness,
a small smile opposite my bench
seeming to come from a faraway land,
a familiar face amidst the unfamiliarity,
ignited a novel passion,
to once again and again start over,
the same monotonous ring of life,
to emulsify that hope,
that hope to delve back into the
oracles of that familiarity.

4. WHISPERS OF A FORGOTTEN BLOOM

My heart thus sings,
amidst the silence of the world,
I wonder,
what beauty thy do not hold,
for the world seeks sustenance
in the illusions of glooming light.
The natural essence of
blooming flowers, the enigmatic
energy of starlit sky,
yet we follow the hollow light
that captures,
yet fails to encapture life.
Following the brackets of order,
circling around the castles in the air,
I wonder,
What beauty thy do not hold,
that we miss the cherry blossoms you behold,
and gleam in the realms
of that that exists but desist.

5. BONDS THAT SPEAK

The eyes met eachother, and stories were shared,
a twinkle of mischief, sparks that flared
between the friends, a silent cue,
of secrets only they knew.
The struggles were real,
To hold the giggles back and conceal
the magic that echoed between them,
From prying eyes and envy that stems
And grows like vineyards, a gossip's strength.

We don't care about the people's decree,
For our love is deeper that what they see,
To being together, in glee and gloom,
The bond we share is a happier doom,
Our lives entwined, like forest canopies,
Creating memories of blissful breeze,
Nothing is dearer than these soulful hours,
for we are writing a story that is ours,
to behold and cherish, a friendship so true.

6. ME, MY BOOK AND A CUP OF COFFEE

The days of sunshine and pristine blue,
Painting the window with a colourful hue,
My eyes search for the rhythmic flow,
Lost in the tale that the author bestows.
A sip of coffee, with whispers of warmth,
Diving into a serene world, an illusion worth,
With smell of ink, like aftermath of rain,
A story in stride, like drizzles on a cycle's chain.
The paucity of time, a pang in the heart,
To leave the pages of truth and depart,
To the dramatic stage, where everything's an act,
Masked in the dreams so abstract.
Yet, just another chance I seek,
To turn just one more page to the end, a mystique,
As I sit there with my book in hand,
To travel to a faraway land.

7. HIDE AND SEEK

My heart is playing hide and seek,
A game I don't understand anymore,
The rules of the game are oblique,
Meant to submerge me to the core,
Failing in each round,
I start counting anew,
But still, I am unable to find,
The feelings that are true,
Each time I deceive myself,
Seeking love, for I misconstrue
The words of manipulation and dispelth,
And drown in the rules of the game untrue,
And still, I continue to play hide and seek,
A game that I don't understand anymore.

8. SHE

A small smile surfaced
Across her bruised face
With pleading eyes she looked up
Not at the wolves who tore her apart
But, at the life she yearned to live,
The dreams she wanted to achieve
And love she had for her country,
She didn't blame anyone
She didn't have the time, she knew,
And she looked around her,
Was it always a safe place for her?
She questioned, not her choice, but her fate,
Tears ran down her cheeks,
Not due to the pain
Causes by the shameless wolves,
But cherishing all her happy moments
That she knows she is going to miss,
she fought against the wolves,
Like a brave leader,
And she won, as her soul left her,

And she wished,
At least once her eyes closed,
The world will open theirs.

9. SILENT STORMS

The small tickles didn't matter to her,
She enjoyed the warmth it held
And smiled at the pinching pain,
She let the breezy wordings flow at her,
Knowing it's price was the joy of others,
As the tickles grew, so did the throb in the heart,
Still did she let it go,
As illusions playing in her heart,
Never did she realize the storm it created in her heart,
As it mushroomed more, like a parasite on her joy,
She silently shouted for it to stop,
But it was too late,
The only thing she could do was let the tears flow
And dry silently...

10. HUES OF LOVE

People say the colour of love is red,
Is it? I ask, what about the moonlit lilac,
The caressing light over its back,
Just like a kiss, a lover's thread.
The smell of the damp earth,
Reminds us of the nutty brown,
A scent that the rain crown
Upon its mate, in whispered breath.
Those who say colour of love is only red,
I pity, for you fail to see the smile,
Of the sun, veiled in bright yellow and orange, while
It hides behind the mountain's spread.
The dreamy black or the yearning green,
an emotion it touches, a love so deep,
no colour defines its measures, for its to keep,
a feeling eternal, pure and serene.

11. SHOWERS OF PARADISE

It is not hard to hear the monosyllables,
for the magic that it resembles,
swirls like little fire crackers,
bursting into silent film of childhood laughter,
reminding us of the memories lost
concealed in a book of frost,
as each drops descended the dramatic stage,
it unfolded the frozen pages of that age,
of innocence and tenderness,
lifting us from emptiness,
transporting us to world of colours and rainbow,
opening that magic window,
evincing the emotions that flow in disguise,
of the rain that showers in paradise.

12. I BELIEVED

All said great to me,
Not a word harsh or rude, I believed;
They applauded with flowers and garlands
I rose high in the sweetness,
Not aware that the flowers were dyed,
Oblivious of the cloned scent, I believed.
In each encore I pictured myself,
Ignorant that they hailed themselves,
I merrily listened to tune of destruction,
Naïve of odious plot I fell into, I believed.
I believed, they toyed with it,
In pace and ploy, they moved forward,
I moved backward, gratified by their fondness,
I was pinched to edge of mountain, I still believed,
I fell.

13. WINGS OF INNOCENCE

I looked at her with conviction,
The glitter in her eyes,
As she waved to the rhythms of innocence,
The little clumsy grace in her moments,
Reminded me of mine,
Of how i struggled to fly as a butterfly,
Those imperfect attempts,
For which I was lauded and praised,
I looked at the little girl,
Dance with dreams in her eyes,
Her lips quivering to the music and
Her limbs moving with freedom,
I wished for that twinkle in her eyes to never fade,
For I knew the pain of getting stuck in spiders web,
With voices questioning my dreams,
Of cutting my wings without hurting them,
I looked at her,
For she reminded me of my twinkle
And prayed,
For her grace not to be saddled into grave.

14. SCARS THAT SPEAK

When the daggers cut right through
The veiled stories that are askew
The blood that drips is not red,
But is invisible, like a cloak that bled
Of the wistful dreams forgotten
In the thread of mistakes, smitten
By the sheen-filled glee it bore,
Ignoring the glory that truth roars,
But remember, the wound is your weapon,
And the pain the beacon,
A lending hand that lifts you,
From the immoral your brew,
Knot your soul to its light,
For it grows the wings for your flight.

15. BROKEN THREADS

The threads that break,
is a mirage of a path untrodden,
A reminder, not to follow the stars that quake,
And tremble, from being sodden,
Due to the melancholic storm.

Don't try to knot those loose threads,
For its strength is weaker than a feather's flare,
Remember, those who try, dreads
For they remain in that frightful air,
In memories of the melancholic storm.

Drenched in the sweat of futile struggle,
To blend the threads in transient union,
Unknown and unaware of the words that fumble,
Just for that one reunion,
That shattered in the melancholic storm.

A life is all you get,
To tread in the clouds of betrayal,

Is a chosen lie, a fateful net,
For understand, it is a hollow trail,
A reminder, not to follow the stars that quake,
Due to the melancholic storm.

16. LOVE YOURSELF

For a moment of pleasure, I say
Place your hand on your heart and stay,
Feel the ensemble of rhythm that flows,
For it is the voice that you behold,
Experience the flutter of your eyelashes,
While you close your eyes,
A starlit ray arise,
That transpose you to the world of hope,
As the air around you hymns,
Realise the enchantedness of your emotions,
The enigmatic beauty of yourself,
And once again listen to the music of your heart,
It prays to love yourself,
For it beholds the pulse of YOU.

17. A HEART'S RUE

She asked me, Are you angry?
Angry? It is an emotion inferior
To the pain I felt and those days wearier,
from the incessant disguise of happiness,
and locking up of fright and sadness,
beneath the fragile sheets of perceived love,
for all I got was silent betrayal and hardened shove.

She asked me, Are you sad?
Sad? Absolutely and undeniably 'Yes'.
But in what magnitude you weigh sadness?
Each tear I shed, could carry the weight of universe,
But, still I waived it as a stranger's curse,
Not your fault, but of a man unknown,
A thing of past, I say, for today, I have grown.

She asked me, can you forgive me?
Forgive you? Always and forever, I will,
But my heart fails to forgive me, still,
For all the wounds I have inflicted, just to love you,

They depict, the thousand times, true,
That I have let it go, just for you,
But, today I want to listen to my heart's rue.

18. LOST

Lost in the bliss of my imagination,
A music caught me by surprise,
It was endowed with a rhythm
Of that dance,
Whose beats I forgot,
Lost in the daily doses of delight,
Those chirping birds
Carried the sound of artful gift
That I once held and let go.
Lost in the hustle-bustle of city
Each light that blinked,
Searched for candlelight that had sparked in me,
Lost in the world that I lost,
I searched vehemently,
To once and again hold that passion,
That ignited my soul,
But I lost all that, unknowingly
Thinking that I gained everything,
And today, I want to hold,

All that I lost, with a hope,
What is lost, can be regained.

19. SECRETS OF THE BLUE

The golden sand of the beach,
Encrusted with pebbles of secrets
With glamour of the waves
Embellishing its body;
Allured my name
And its soft shouts pronounced
Words of serenity,
As if the waves wished to tell me
The secrets that it beheld,
Of the seraphic beauty of the shore,
The silver linings of the wave,
Of its dancing shells and
The life that shines deep within,
The magic of the blues, I felt like
Each soft bellow of the waves
Was enthralled to tell me
The secrets of the blue.

20. VERSES OF LIBERATION

Those words of fiction were true,
An unfinished story yet new,
A longingness to feel the magic of the air,
Of love that wraps around, and lift me from mortal flare
To the enigmatic life of soulful gaze,
Of roses, swords and fantastical maze.
A drift from the monster of realities,
To join the tale of verity, far away from the dualities
That lurk between hope and fear,
To once, just enjoy and cheer,
Those words of burning desire,
Of that which is unknown, but not dire.
These verses, are not just falling letters,
They are liberation from daunting fetters,
Of that which curtailed mind, an inner stride,
Reigniting the reader's pride,
Of that unfinished story yet new,
As those words of fiction were true.

21. THE CANVAS OF DREAMS

Each stroke of an artistic mirror,
Is a blend of colours, a journey within,
That shows us the magic we hold,
An appreciation of our shining soul.
The glimmering surface is a reflection closer
Of the dreams held dearer, and to begin
A voyage, to grab that medal of gold,
To rise above and achieve that goal.

Each stroke of an artistic mirror,
Is an emblem of those tireless pursuits
That resonates the passion in your eyes,
To fight and fight back, and win.
These days of endless struggle, is a path clearer,
A shooting star to remain resolute,
To not just wish, but rise beyond the skies,
And to meet your mirror with a joyful grin.

Thus, again I say, each stroke of an artistic mirror,

Is reflection of YOU, and your Shining soul,
To win the maze of life,
And rise like a phoenix again.

www.ingramcontent.com/pod-product-compliance
Lightning Source LLC
Chambersburg PA
CBHW071237140726
47996CB00007B/2644